TY BARKER

Data Analytics Made Simple

A Beginner's Blueprint into Tech

Copyright © 2024 by Ty Barker

All rights reserved. No part of this publication may be reproduced, stored or transmitted in any form or by any means, electronic, mechanical, photocopying, recording, scanning, or otherwise without written permission from the publisher. It is illegal to copy this book, post it to a website, or distribute it by any other means without permission.

First edition

This book was professionally typeset on Reedsy.
Find out more at reedsy.com

Contents

Prologue	1
Introduction	3
Purpose of the Book	3
Who This Book Is For	3
My Story	4
What Readers Will Learn	4
1 Understanding Data Analytics	5
What is Data Analytics?	5
Why Does Data Analytics Matters?	7
Types of Data Analytics	8
Career Opportunities	9
2 Breaking Misconceptions	11
You Don't Need a Computer Science Degree	11
Coding vs. No-Code Skills	12
It's Affordable to Learn	13
3 Tools and Skills You Need to Learn	15
Core Tools for Beginners	15
Key Skills	16
How to Learn These Tools	17
4 Hands-On Practice	20
Building Your Portfolio	20
Step-by-Step Projects to Showcase Skills	21
Where to Find Free Datasets	22
Documenting Your Work	23

5 Landing Your First Data Analyst Role	25
Building Your Resume	25
Where to Find Entry-Level Jobs	27
Preparing for Interviews	29
Getting Experience Without a Job	31
6 Conclusion	33
Understanding Data Analytics	34
Learning Tools and Core Skills	34
Building Projects and Showcasing Them	34
Landing an Entry-Level Role	35
7 Thank You for Reading!	37
8 Resources	38

Prologue

When I first decided to become a data analyst, I felt overwhelmed by the mass amounts information, tools, and skills to learn all over the internet. It make it seem like an impossible mountain to climb. I didn't have a degree in computer science, nor did I have years of tech experience. But I what i did have was curiosity, determination, and a desire to change my career and my life.

As I took my first steps into the world of data analytics, I quickly realized that the path isn't always clear and it doesn't have to be. This is a field that is constantly growing, driven by interest and creativity as much as by technical skill. I learned that with the right resources, dedication, and a willingness to learn, anyone can break into this industry and thrive.

This book is a combination of everything I've learned on my journey to becoming a successful Data Analyst. It's a guide for people just like you, whether you're considering a career change, new to the workforce, or just interested in what data analytics has to offer.

My goal is to simplify the process, eliminate the stress , and show you that becoming a data analyst isn't about when you start, but about where you're willing to go. This book is more than just a road map it's proof that you can do it, too.

So, take a seat, open your mind, and get ready to dive into the world of data . Whether you're here to land your dream job in tech, expand your skills, or just learn something new, you're in the right place.

Let's begin your journey into the rewarding world of data analytics.

Introduction

Purpose of the Book

The purpose of this book is because when I started my journey to become a data analyst, I wished I had a mentor or a clear step by step guide to follow. The trial and error I went through could have easily been avoided with someone pointing me in the right direction . So My goal in writing this book is to offer the help I never got to other aspiring data analysts. I want to show them that it's never too late to switch careers and pursue a fulfilling path in tech.

Who This Book Is For

This book is for young adults who chose not to attend college or for someone who is reentering the workforce, or just anyone looking to refresh their knowledge of data analysis. It's especially helpful for those who do not have any coding experience and want a clear and easily accessible guide to breaking into the field of data analytics.

My Story

A few years ago, I got an injury that shattered my dreams of pursuing my ideal career. You know parents always want you to become a doctor or a lawyer. So This was really hard for me, especially since I had always seen this path for myself for as long as I could remember. I felt defeated and unclear about what to do as a career in my future. So I started dancing down several different career paths and one day while scrolling online, I stumbled upon data analysis as a potential career path, and something about it caught my interest. Since I have always been good with computers and a very quick study , I started on this training as well as I did with the others. I started experimenting with online data cleaning mini-courses, and to my surprise, I was really good at it. After a year of trial and error, I landed my first freelance data gig and the rest was history.

What Readers Will Learn

In this book, you will get a clear layout and step by step blueprint into data to get you from not knowing anything about data analytics to clearly understanding and being able to find and use (free and affordable) tools in order to become a great data analyst. You will learn the basic tools for data analysis, including Excel, SQL, and data visualization, with no need for coding. You will also understand how to build your own portfolio with hands-on projects, how to land your first data analyst job or gig ,and how to start your career path with a straightforward, practical plan.

1

Understanding Data Analytics

What is Data Analytics?

Data analytics, simply put, is the process of examining raw data to uncover patterns, trends, and important insights that help people and businesses make smarter choices.

Let's choose an example you may use everyday like Netflix. When you open the app, the first thing you see are recommendations personalized just for you. You may wonder how Netflix knows what to suggest? They look at the shows and movies you have already watched, analyze that data, and identify patterns to predict what you're likely to enjoy next. By doing this, Netflix increases the chances that you'll find something you like, keeping you engaged, entertained, and continuing to pay for your subscription with them.

Another example is budgeting apps, like Albert or Mint. These apps connect to your bank account and analyze your spending habits. They can find trends, like how much you're spending on dining out or subscriptions. If you're overspending or paying for something twice (like two streaming services you forgot about), the app will flag it and suggest ways to minimize your spending. This can help you manage your money better, save for big goals, or free up extra cash.

In both cases, data analytics is working behind the scenes to make life easier: Netflix helps you discover shows you'll love, and budgeting apps help you make better financial choices.

Aside from everyday life, data analytics works in areas like health, education, and transportation. For example:

- **Health**: Fitness trackers like FitBit analyze your activity and heart rate to provide a better understanding of your overall health.
- **Education**: Schools analyze data of students' grades to find areas where students need extra help and improve teaching methods so they can become better academically.
- **Transportation**: Apps like Google Maps or Waze collect and analyze traffic data in real time to show you the fastest route to your destination and avoid slower roads.

The magic of data analytics is in its ability to turn numbers into knowledge. Whether it's finding a new show to binge, helping you save money, or getting you to your destination faster, data analytics improves everyday decisions in ways you might not even notice. By examining patterns and trends, it helps businesses succeed, individuals improve their lives, and entire industries create and grow for a better future.

Why Does Data Analytics Matters?

Data analytics matters because it helps businesses grow, improve, and make smarter, more profitable decisions. But data analytics isn't just for businesses it's everywhere, quietly shaping our lives and making things easier.

Think about when you're tracking your steps on a Fitbit. The device collects data about how much you walk, your heart rate, and even your sleep patterns. By analyzing this information, it provides insights to help you move more, sleep better, and improve your overall health.

Or let's say you're watching an item online, waiting for the price to drop. Websites track data like how many people are viewing the product, how often it's purchased, and seasonal trends. By analyzing this, they decide when to lower the price and you get notified when it happens, saving you money.

Another example is checking when the next bus arrives. Apps like Google Maps or transit trackers analyze real time data from GPS signals to give you up to date information, so you know exactly when to leave and avoid waiting at the bus stop for too long.

In industries like healthcare, sports, and education, data analytics is transforming how we solve problems and make progress:

- **Healthcare**: Doctors and hospitals use patient data to predict disease patterns, personalize treatments, and improve outcomes.
- **Sports**: Coaches analyze player performance, team stats, and game strategies to improve training and win more games.

- **Education**: Schools analyze student progress to identify learning gaps, improve teaching methods, and boost student success.

Simply put, data analytics helps make sense of the world around us. It takes large amounts of unfiltered information, organizes it, to find meaningful patterns. Whether it's improving your health, saving you money, or helping companies solve big problems, data analytics helps us to make better decisions, better our lives, and create meaningful change.

Types of Data Analytics

There are four main types of data analytics, each have a specific and important role in helping businesses and individuals make educated decisions based on data.

- **Descriptive Analytics** focuses on what happened in the past. For example, it might involve tracking sales numbers, website traffic, or customer activity over a certain period of time.
- **Diagnostic Analytics** explains why something happened. This could include identifying the reasons behind a decline in sales or why users stopped engaging with a product.
- **Predictive Analytics** is used to predict what is likely to happen in the future. Businesses use it to predict customer behavior, market trends, or future sales.
- **Prescriptive Analytics** recommends specific actions to take in order to influence future outcomes. For instance, it might suggest the best pricing strategy or marketing approach to

maximize profits.

These four types of data analytics make a clear framework for understanding, explaining, predicting, and making business decisions. Whether it's a small business, a healthcare professional, or a marketing agency, all of these analytical ideas can provide important value that helps improve efficiency, increase profitability, and achieve long-term success.

Career Opportunities

Data analytics knowledge opens the door to many different career opportunities within all different industries.It can be a field you already work in just a different department. Here are some of the most common roles you can pursue and what they focus on.

- **Data Analyst:** Focuses on interpreting and analyzing data to provide actionable insights for businesses.
- **Business Analyst:** Bridges the gap between business needs and technology solutions, using data to drive strategic decisions.
- **Data Engineer:** Builds and maintains the system needed to store, process, and manage large datasets.
- **Data Visualization Engineer:** Specializes in creating dashboards and visual tools that make complex data easy to understand.
- **Data Governance Analyst:** Ensures data is secure, accurate, and follows all regulations.
- **Risk Analyst:** Identifies and analyzes potential risks to help

organizations make safer decisions.
- **Quantitative Analyst:** Uses mathematical models to analyze data, often in financial markets.
- **Financial Analyst:** Focuses on analyzing financial data to help businesses make investment and budgeting decisions.
- **Marketing Analytics Manager:** Uses data to evaluate marketing strategies and grow campaigns for better results.
- **Business Intelligence Analyst:** Designs tools and reports to help organizations track performance and identify opportunities.
- **Data Scientist:** Uses advanced techniques like machine learning and statistical modeling to solve complex problems and forecast future trends.

No matter your interests or background, there's more than likely a role in data analytics that aligns with your skill set and goals.

2

Breaking Misconceptions

You Don't Need a Computer Science Degree

When I first decided to get into data analytics, I thought I would need a degree that would take 2-4 years to complete. But as I started looking into universities and programs, thinking that was the only path to enter the field. I came across a link that introduced me to data analytics boot camps that could be completed in as little as six months. That was an absolute game changer. I realized that you don't need to commit to years of school or even pursue a computer science degree to start a career in data analytics.

In fact, many people break into the field without a formal degree by using alternative learning resources. Some even turn to "YouTube University" to gather the knowledge they need, learning from countless free videos and tutorials. I personally have spent hours sifting through content to figure out what skills I needed to learn, and let me tell you, the information is out there you just need to know where to look. Whether it's blogs, YouTube channels, or online forums, there is an abundance of free resources that can teach you the fundamentals of data analysis.

Online platforms like Coursera and even Google's Data Analytics Certification program offer structured learning without the hefty price tag of a traditional degree. The key is being committed and staying consistent. You don't need to spend years in a classroom, if you're willing to put in the time and effort, you can gain the skills needed to become a proficient data analyst in less than half of the time it would take to earn a degree.

Coding vs. No-Code Skills

One of the biggest misconceptions about becoming a data analyst is that you need to know how to code. The truth is, many of the fundamental tools used in data analytics don't require any coding experience at all.

Programs like Excel, Power BI, and Tableau allow you to analyze, visualize, and interpret data without writing a single line of code. With Excel, for example, you can clean and organize data, perform calculations, and create charts to uncover insights. Tools like Tableau and Power BI make it easy to turn complex data into interactive dashboards and reports with simple drag and drop features.

That said, learning to code can help you expand your skills as you advance in your career, but it's not required to get started.

Many successful data analysts begin with no code tools, gain confidence, and then decide whether to add coding languages to their toolkit later.

In short, you can become a great data analyst using no code tools alone, so don't let the idea of coding hold you back from getting started.

It's Affordable to Learn

Once you realize that you don't need a degree or coding experience to break into the tech field, the next common misconception is that it costs a fortune to learn the necessary skills. While some resources can be pricey, the truth is that most learning opportunities are either low cost or completely free and they can still provide you with everything you need to become a successful data analyst.

One of the best free ways to gain experience, especially if you're a recent graduate or someone reentering the workforce, is through internships or apprenticeships. These opportunities are invaluable for gaining hands-on skills and building your portfolio.

If you're self motivated, platforms like YouTube offer a wealth of free tutorials that cover everything from data cleaning to visualization techniques. Additionally, online bootcamps often provide structured programs that guide you step by step, many of which are affordable.

For me, I decided to go with a low cost option: the Google Data Analytics Certificate on Coursera. At just $50 a month, it was an investment that fit my budget and gave me the foundation I needed to start working in the field. Plus, Coursera offers free resources and trials for many of its courses, making it accessible to anyone eager to learn.

Whether you choose free YouTube videos, an affordable certification program, or an internship, there's a path to data analytics that won't break the bank. With so many options available, starting your journey is more attainable than you might think.

3

Tools and Skills You Need to Learn

Core Tools for Beginners

When starting your journey as a data analyst, you don't need to master every tool under the sun. Instead, focus on a few essential tools that are beginner-friendly and widely used in the industry.

1. **Excel/Google** Sheets Excel and Google Sheets are the starting points for most data analysts. These tools allow you to organize, clean, and analyze data using formulas, pivot tables, and charts. They're simple to learn and powerful enough for many tasks.
2. **SQL (Basic Queries)** SQL, or Structured Query Language, is used to retrieve and manipulate data stored in databases. Learning basic queries like SELECT, WHERE, and JOIN can

help you work with large datasets effectively. It's a must-have skill for anyone looking to analyze data in a business setting.
3. **Data Visualization Tools: Tableau and Power** Bi Tools like Tableau and Power BI make it easy to turn raw data into meaningful visuals like charts, graphs, and dashboards. These tools require no coding and are essential for presenting your findings in a clear and compelling way.
4. **R**R is a popular programming language for statistical analysis and data visualization. While not mandatory for beginners, learning the basics of R can expand your ability to analyze complex data and perform advanced calculations.
5. **Python for** Beginners Python is a versatile programming language often used in data analytics for tasks like automation, data cleaning, and machine learning. It's optional when you're just starting out but can be a great tool to learn as you advance in your career.

By focusing on these core tools, you'll gain a solid foundation in data analytics without feeling overwhelmed. Start small, practice consistently, and build your skills one step at a time.

Key Skills

To succeed as a data analyst, you need to build a strong foundation in a few essential skills. These skills will help you turn raw data into valuable insights that drive smart decisions.

1. **Understanding Data: Cleaning and** Organizing Raw data

is often messy and unstructured. One of the first things you'll learn as a data analyst is how to clean and organize data. This involves removing duplicates, handling missing values, and formatting the data so it's ready for analysis. Clean data is the backbone of accurate results.
2. **Creating Reports and** Dashboards As a data analyst, you'll need to present your findings in a way that others can easily understand. Tools like Tableau, Power BI, or Excel allow you to create visually appealing reports and interactive dashboards that highlight key trends and metrics. Clear visuals make your insights easily understandable for business owners.
3. **Analyzing Trends and Drawing** Insights Beyond organizing and presenting data, your main role as an analyst is to interpret it. This means identifying patterns, analyzing trends, and drawing meaningful conclusions that help businesses make informed decisions. For example, you might analyze sales data to identify which products are performing well or predict future trends based on past performance.

By mastering these key skills, data cleaning, report creation, and analysis, you'll have everything you need to add value as a data analyst and contribute to data driven success.

How to Learn These Tools

There are many great resources available for learning the core tools of data analytics. Whether you're just starting out or looking to deepen your knowledge, the following websites offer excellent free or low-cost courses and tutorials to help you develop your skills:

1. **W3Schools SQL Tutorial** W3Schools is a fantastic resource for learning SQL. It offers beginner-friendly tutorials and practice exercises that will help you get comfortable with basic SQL queries.https://www.w3schools.com/sql/
2. **Coursera** Coursera offers a variety of affordable courses on data analytics, including the Google Data Analytics Certificate. You can access some courses for free or pay for a certification at a low monthly rate.https://www.coursera.org/
3. **DataCamp** DataCamp is another great platform with hands-on courses on data analysis, SQL, R, and Python. While they offer paid plans, there are free introductory courses available.https://www.datacamp.com/
4. **Kaggle Learn** Kaggle offers free, interactive tutorials that help you build your skills in data analysis, machine learning, and more. They also have datasets you can practice on, making it a great place to apply what you learn.https://www.kaggle.com/learn
5. **YouTube** YouTube is a treasure trove of free tutorials on data analytics. Simply search for "data analyst skills" to find a variety of beginner-friendly videos. https://www.youtube.com/results?search_query=data+analyst+skills
6. **SQLZoo** SQL (Structured Query Language) is a key skill for data analysts. Use SQLZoo to learn the basics of SQL queries, from simple SELECT statements to more complex joins and subqueries.https://sqlzoo.net/

By exploring these resources, you'll be able to start learning the necessary tools without spending a lot of money. Dive into one or more of these sites and begin building your skills today!

4

Hands-On Practice

Building Your Portfolio

As a beginner, having a portfolio is one of the most important steps you can take to demonstrate your skills and commitment as a data analyst. Since you may not have a formal degree to show employers, your portfolio becomes your proof that you have obtained the necessary skills and are prepared for the job.

Think of it this way: If an artist told you, "I'm great at painting, pay me to paint for your gallery," you'd probably want to see some of their artwork first, right? The same applies to data analysts. Without a degree, you need a portfolio that showcases your ability to handle real-world data, analyze it, and present actionable insights.

Your portfolio doesn't have to be huge or complicated. In fact, it's better to start small and gradually build up as you gain more experience. You can include projects like:

- Cleaning and analyzing a public dataset
- Creating visual reports and dashboards
- Performing data analysis for a mock business case

A strong portfolio will not only help you stand out to potential employers but also build your confidence as you complete real-world projects.

Step-by-Step Projects to Showcase Skills

As I mentioned earlier, it's best to start small and build your skills gradually. One of the simplest ways to begin is with spreadsheets in Excel. Find or create datasets from your own life like your monthly spending and use them to calculate sums, averages, and create charts and graphs. This hands-on approach will help you gain confidence in your skills and get comfortable with the basics. It's exactly how I got started.

Here's a breakdown of step by step projects to help you showcase your skills:

Project 1: Analyze Sales Data in Excel

Create a simple dataset or find one online, such as sales data, and practice analyzing it using Excel. Calculate totals, averages, and any other statistics you think are important. Use Excel's built-in tools to create charts and graphs to visually represent the data. This will help you become familiar with data analysis and visualization techniques in a tool that's widely used in the industry.

Project 2: Write Basic SQL Queries to Pull Data

Start with learning SQL, a fundamental skill for any data analyst. Use free platforms like SQLZoo to practice writing basic SQL queries. This project will help you understand how to retrieve and manipulate data from a database.

Project 3: Build a Visualization in Tableau/Power BI

Once you've worked with Excel and SQL, the next step is creating more advanced visualizations. Use Tableau or Power BI to build a visualization with a sample dataset, like global population trends or sales performance data. These tools will help you create professional looking reports and dashboards that effectively communicate your analysis.

By completing these projects, you'll build a strong foundation in data analysis and visualization, which will be crucial for your portfolio.

Where to Find Free Datasets

During my journey, one of the best resources I found for free datasets was Kaggle. Not only does Kaggle have a huge variety of datasets for every kind of analysis, but it also has a supportive community where you can ask questions, share your projects, and learn from others. It's a great place to start if you're looking for real-world data to practice with.

Here are some other great places to find free datasets:

1. **Kaggle** – Offers datasets for every level of data analysis, from beginner to expert. You can also participate in competitions to challenge yourself and improve your skills.https://www.kaggle.com/datasets

2. **Google Dataset Search** – A tool from Google to help you find publicly available datasets from around the web.https://datasetsearch.research.google.com/
3. **Data.gov** – A comprehensive resource for U.S. government data, offering free datasets in areas like education, health, science, and transportation.https://www.data.gov/
4. **UCI Machine Learning Repository** – A collection of databases, domain theories, and datasets often used for machine learning research and practice.https://archive.ics.uci.edu/ml/index.php
5. **FiveThirtyEight** – Provides datasets related to politics, sports, science, and economics, often used to power their data-driven stories.https://github.com/fivethirtyeight/data

These platforms offer a wide variety of datasets for you to practice and apply your skills to, no matter what area of data analysis you're interested in.

Documenting Your Work

Documenting your work is key to showing potential employers that you have the skills to back up your claims. For me, Kaggle was one of the first places where I started sharing analysis from both my personal life and datasets I found online. It's a great platform for not only practicing your skills but also showcasing your work to a global community.

One of the best ways to make your portfolio visible to employers is by linking it to your LinkedIn profile. This way, when employers view your profile, they can see your projects, datasets, and the skills you've applied to real-world data. It's a powerful way to demonstrate your experience without a degree.

I also personally use my own blog to share my datasets and the projects I'm working on. This has been a great way to keep myself motivated while providing an avenue for my audience to connect with me. It's a space where I can share my personal experiences and show the process of my learning journey.

Here are some tips on how to effectively showcase your projects:

1. **LinkedIn**: Add links to your completed projects, including descriptions of what you did and what skills you used. Regularly update your profile to reflect your most recent work.
2. **GitHub**: Create a repository for each project, including detailed descriptions of what each project entails. GitHub is a great tool for displaying your work to technical employers.
3. **Personal Blog**: Share the datasets you've worked on, write about your analysis process, and offer insights on how you solved problems. This is an excellent way to show both your technical and communication skills.

Sharing your work and showcasing it on multiple platforms will give you more visibility and credibility. It also keeps you motivated and helps you build an online presence, which is critical when you're breaking into a new field.

5

Landing Your First Data Analyst Role

Building Your Resume

A common misconception is that when transitioning into a data analyst role, you have to completely erase your previous experience or that without direct experience in data analysis, you won't be able to land a job. Both of these ideas are far from true. The skills you've gained from other jobs, even if they aren't directly related to data analysis, can be framed in a way that shows employers you already have valuable transferable skills.

Remember, data analysis is used in many areas of life from budgeting to improving business processes. You just need to highlight the skills you've used in other roles and relate them to the field. For example, if you've worked in customer service, you might have experience with identifying trends in customer behavior. Or, if you've worked in finance, you may already have experience with data analysis in managing budgets or forecasting.

How to format your portfolio-centered resume:

1. **Focus on Relevant Skills**: Even if you don't have formal data analyst experience, list the skills you've developed from previous roles that are applicable. Think about your proficiency with tools like Excel, SQL, Power BI, or any other relevant software. Also include soft skills like problem-solving, communication, and attention to detail, these are useful in the data role as well.
2. **Include Certifications and Courses**: If you've completed certifications (like Google's Data Analytics certification or courses on platforms like Coursera, DataCamp, or Kaggle), make sure these are clearly displayed on your resume. These show your commitment to learning and your understanding of essential tools and concepts.
3. **Showcase Projects**: Highlight personal or freelance projects you've worked on in your portfolio. These projects prove that you can apply the skills you've learned to real-world problems. Be specific about the tasks you completed, such as cleaning data, creating dashboards, or analyzing trends.
4. **Resume Formatting Tips**:

- **Header**: Include your name, contact information, and LinkedIn/GitHub/blog links at the top.
- **Summary or Objective**: Write a brief section about your career transition, emphasizing your enthusiasm for data analysis and your transferable skills.

- **Skills Section**: List key tools and techniques, such as Excel, SQL, Power BI, Tableau, data visualization, etc.
- **Experience Section**: Describe past roles, but tailor your bullet points to highlight any relevant data-related tasks.
- **Education and Certifications**: List any relevant certifications or formal education you've completed.
- **Portfolio**: Include a link to your online portfolio (LinkedIn, GitHub, personal blog) where employers can see your projects in detail.

By focusing on your skills, certifications, and projects, you can effectively build a data analyst resume that showcases your qualifications, even if you're just starting out in the field.

Where to Find Entry-Level Jobs

Finding entry-level data analyst jobs can be a challenge, but the key is to actively search and put yourself out there. Many people shy away from applying to jobs they think they're not qualified for, but if you're serious about breaking into data analytics, you can't let fear hold you back.

One of the biggest mistakes aspiring analysts make is looking at traditional job boards, like Indeed, and seeing that most jobs require a bachelor's or master's degree. Apply anyway. Even if the job listing asks for a degree you don't have, still submit your application. When you get to the section where they ask if you have anything else to add, include a link to your portfolio. Trust me, employers will appreciate that you're showing them your real-world skills and not just relying on a degree.

The best job board for finding entry-level roles is LinkedIn. You can search for jobs, but you should also actively network.

Make sure your profile is always up to date and includes all your certifications, skills, and a link to your portfolio. Many hiring managers use LinkedIn to find potential candidates, so it's a great way to get noticed.

Another option that worked for me is applying for apprenticeships. After completing my Google Certificate, I signed up for a data analytics apprenticeship, and it turned out to be the best route. Apprenticeships give you the opportunity to gain hands-on experience while following experienced analysts, which can help you learn and grow in real-time. Plus, apprenticeships are usually paid, so you're earning while learning, and the experience could lead to a full-time job.

There are also internships available in data analytics. While internships are often unpaid, they can offer invaluable experience and networking opportunities that can lead to a full-time role in the future.

Job boards to check

- **Indeed**: Look for entry-level roles, and apply even if you don't meet every requirement.
- **LinkedIn**: Great for finding jobs and networking with professionals in the field.
- **Glassdoor**: Another job board to find positions and read reviews about companies.

Entry-level opportunities

- **Apprenticeships**: Paid, hands-on learning opportunities that could lead to a full-time position.
- **Internships**: Sometimes unpaid but excellent for gaining experience and networking.

By putting yourself out there on job boards and seeking out apprenticeships or internships, you'll increase your chances of landing your first data analyst job. Don't let the qualifications listed on job postings intimidate you and show employers what you can do with a strong portfolio and a proactive attitude!

Preparing for Interviews

Interviewing for jobs in the tech field can feel intimidating, especially when you start getting nervous and experience brain fog. But let me tell you there's no need to be anxious. You've already put in the work, learned the necessary skills, and built a portfolio that showcases your abilities. Now, it's just about showing employers what you can do in person.

One common part of data analyst interviews is the case study. Employers often ask you to complete a case study during the interview, where you'll need to explain your thought process and how you would approach a real-world data problem. This is exactly what you've been practicing! It's just a matter of putting your skills into words and explaining them to the interviewer. You've done this work before with your projects now, it's time to show them your approach.

Don't worry about nerves, shake them off and remind yourself that you're prepared. You've done the research, learned the tools, and completed projects that demonstrate your capability. Now, it's just about explaining your process clearly and confidently.

For other interview questions that you may be asked, there are plenty of resources to help you prepare. One great resource is YouTube University. There are many videos that list common data analyst interview questions and provide advice on how to

answer them. One useful video you can watch is this one on 66 sample questions and answers:https://youtu.be/Y6175TGFuMI
Here's how you can prepare for your interview:

1. **Showcase your projects**: Make sure you highlight the work you've done and how it's relevant to the role. Explain the steps you took, the challenges you faced, and how you overcame them. Employers love to hear about your problem solving process.
2. **Be ready to explain your thought process**: When completing case studies, explain your reasoning for each step you take. Show that you understand the data and can draw actionable insights from it.
3. **Prepare for behavioral questions**: These are questions that focus on your previous experiences and how you handle challenges, teamwork, and other aspects of your professional life. Practice answering these types of questions using the **STAR method** (Situation, Task, Action, Result).
4. **Ask questions**: Don't forget that an interview is also your chance to assess if the company is the right fit for you. Prepare a few questions about the team, the company's approach to data, or their expectations for the role.

Remember, the goal of the interview is not just to prove you can do the job but to show your enthusiasm and ability to communicate your findings clearly. Employers want someone who can not only perform technical tasks but also share insights with others effectively.

Getting Experience Without a Job

Lack of work experience whether in general or specifically in tech does not mean you're shut out from opportunities. As I mentioned earlier, the skills you've gained and the portfolio you've built can often speak louder than traditional experience or a degree. But if you're eager to build some hands-on experience, there are plenty of ways to do so.

One way to gain experience is through freelance work. Start by reaching out to small businesses or startups that may not have the budget for large data teams but still need help with data related projects. Offer to complete a one week project to build their reports, clean their data, or analyze their trends. This way, you can showcase your skills while contributing to real-world tasks.

Another option is to volunteer your skills for family members, friends, or non-profits that might benefit from some data work. Many small organizations and individuals need help with organizing or analyzing their data but may not have the budget for a full-time analyst. Volunteering in these situations allows you to gain real-world experience while also helping others.

Additionally, personal data challenges are a great way to keep your skills fresh and continue learning. These can be small projects based on data from your own life or public datasets that you work through on your own. For example, you might track and analyze your monthly spending, set up a fitness tracking project, or look at trends in online data sources. Doing this regularly will help you stay sharp and motivated while you're looking for job opportunities.

By staying active and involved in data work, you'll continue to sharpen your skills and increase your confidence, making it easier to land the next opportunity.

6

Conclusion

Congratulations! You now have a clear roadmap to start your journey toward becoming a data analyst, no matter the path you choose. This guide has provided you with the essential steps, skills, and strategies needed to break into the tech field. You have a solid understanding of what the role entails, the key tools and knowledge required, and where to access them to succeed. You also know how to build a strong portfolio to showcase your abilities to potential employers. With this guidance, you're well-equipped to take meaningful steps toward landing the perfect job that aligns with your personal goals and aspirations in the tech industry.

Understanding Data Analytics

You now know what data analytics is all about the process of analyzing raw data to extract meaningful insights that help make informed business decisions. You've learned about the different types of analytics (descriptive, diagnostic, predictive, and prescriptive) and how they are used across various industries to solve problems, predict trends, and guide strategic decisions. With this foundational knowledge, you can confidently navigate the world of data analytics and see its importance in everything from business growth to healthcare and sports.

Learning Tools and Core Skills

As a data analyst, you'll work with a variety of tools, but you don't need to be intimidated by the prospect of learning complex software. We've broken it down into manageable steps, starting with the most important and accessible tools. You've learned how to work with Excel/Google Sheets, SQL, Tableau, Power BI, and the basics of R tools that don't require coding expertise at the start. You've also been introduced to platforms like YouTube, Coursera, and Kaggle, where you can find both free and affordable resources to help you build your skills. By focusing on mastering these tools, you'll develop the ability to clean, analyze, and visualize data effectively.

Building Projects and Showcasing Them

One of the most important things you can do as a beginner is to build a portfolio. Your portfolio will serve as tangible proof of your abilities, helping you stand out to employers and demonstrate your practical skills. Whether you start with small projects in Excel or dive into visualizations in Tableau and Power BI, every project you complete adds value to your portfolio. Remember, the key is to showcase your work through platforms like LinkedIn, GitHub, or a personal blog. These projects not only help you build confidence, but they also provide real world examples that employers will be looking for when assessing your abilities.

Landing an Entry-Level Role

Lastly, now that you've built your skills and portfolio, it's time to start looking for an entry-level job in data analytics. As you embark on your job search, remember that perseverance and self-promotion are key. Apply for jobs even if you don't meet every single requirement, and don't be afraid to showcase your portfolio during the application process. Consider internships, apprenticeships, and freelance work to gain valuable experience while continuing to learn. Platforms like LinkedIn and Indeed are great job boards to find opportunities.

You're now ready to take the next step with confidence. You have the skills, the portfolio, and the knowledge to land that first job and begin your career as a data analyst. Keep pushing forward, and remember that the journey is as important as the destination. Each step you take brings you closer to your goal. The tech field is full of opportunities, and with dedication, you'll be able to carve out a path that aligns with your passions and ambitions.

Now, go ahead and take the first step you're ready to succeed in data analytics!

The best way to get started is to take that first step. Don't worry about mastering everything right away, start small, but start somewhere! Whether it's learning the basics of Excel, experimenting with a simple dataset in Google Sheets, or building your first visualization in Tableau, every small effort will add up over time.

The key is to get started today. The faster you dive in, the faster you'll grow. You can become a data wiz. It's all about taking consistent action and learning along the way. Pick a tool or project today, and start building your skills. You've got this!

The journey to becoming a data analyst begins with just one step so go ahead and take it!

7

Thank You for Reading!

If you found any value in this book, I would greatly appreciate it if you could take a moment to leave a review on Amazon. Your feedback not only helps me improve but also helps others on their journey to becoming a data analyst.

I would love to hear your thoughts, experiences, or how this guide has helped you.

Thank you again for reading, and I wish you the very best as you embark on your exciting journey to becoming a Data Analyst.

Keep learning, keep growing, and keep analyzing!

8

Resources

CareerFoundry. (n.d.). *What is data analytics?* CareerFoundry. https://careerfoundry.com/en/blog/data-analytics/what-is-data-analytics/#what-is-data-analytics

DataCamp. (2023, February 21). *Top ten analytics careers.* DataCamp. https://www.datacamp.com/blog/top-ten-analytics-careers

Indeed. (n.d.). *Job search.* Indeed. https://www.indeed.com/

Insightsoftware. (2020, August 19). *Comparing descriptive, predictive, prescriptive, and diagnostic analytics.* insightsoftware. https://insightsoftware.com/blog/comparing-descriptive-predictive-prescriptive-and-diagnostic-analytics/#:~:text=Descriptive%20Analytics%20tells%20you%20what,take%20to%20affect%20those%20outcomes

Simplilearn. (n.d.). *Data analyst interview questions.* Simplilearn. https://www.simplilearn.com/tutorials/data-analytics-tutorial/data-analyst-interview-questions

www.ingramcontent.com/pod-product-compliance
Lightning Source LLC
Chambersburg PA
CBHW070951220526
45471CB00007B/2989